Overcoming against all odds

...A story of Blind Faith...

□

June Russell

Dedicated to those who need the reality of a living hope as they go through the storms of life.

ISBN 978-1-4717-3440-3

Email: jrussell@lifeinthekingdom.co.uk
or write to:

June Russell
Life in the Kingdom
PO Box 66289
London
SW6 9FE

'O you afflicted, storm-tossed
and not comforted,
behold I will set your stones
in fair colours and lay your
foundations with sapphires.'

Isaiah 54:11

ACKNOWLEDGEMENTS

The Bible tells us that Jesus is the vine, we are the branches. If we abide in Him, and He in us, we will bear much fruit; for without Him we can do nothing. John 15:5

This book came as a result of inspiration of the Holy Spirit alone. He gave me the desire to write and opened up the scriptures to me. I praise the Lord for this wonderful gift and all the glory must go to Him for what He will do in and through the lives of those who read it.

I would like to thank and acknowledge the O'Brien family. Laurence who feely gave of his time and talents to ensure that I would become a published author. Laura his wife and his mother Jo for the time and effort they put into spelling and grammar checks of the book.

Many thanks also go to Brother Rudy Brann for his encouragement from six years earlier. He was the first to support my potential by sowing seed and purchasing copies of my books in their raw form to give away to others. Brother Rudy also gave of his precious time to edit this and other books which I have written.

Grateful thanks to Mrs Merle Aqui for her staunch support of my writing gift and her faithfulness in the area of encouragement and believing in me.

The wonderful picture on the front cover was designed for this book in the year 2000 by the much talented and gifted Mark Dishley and I glorify God for his gift.

CONTENTS

FOREWORD

DON'T GIVE UP OR GIVE IN!

Sometimes my walk as a Christian feels that I am on the outside looking in. I feel misunderstood and ignored. I related to Bartimaeus, the central character of this book, a blind man who was passed by, ignored, unnoticed and insignificant. I have certainly had feelings of isolation and detachment.

In chapter 7 of the book there is a part which says "who are you to call on Jesus he won't help you." There have definitely been times in my life where I have been mocked with those same words.

Jesus doesn't care about your past, whatever it is He has compassion and loves you no matter what. Jesus loves outcasts and all those rejected by society.

It strikes me that Bartimaeus was blind with blinkers of faith on when it came to Jesus. He only Saw blind faith. I was led to imagine the multitudes and hoards of people all around him. It must have been scary being a blind man in a huge crowd. All he wanted was to be touched by Jesus. In all of that commotion he was heard above all of that noise because his cries were so heartfelt and so real.

Bartimaeus made the decision to just reach out in faith and throw aside his garment (baggage). How many times have I decided to move forward and throw off the baggage of life only to go back later and pick it up? I admired Bartimaeus. When he made that decision he threw his past behind him and left it there.

Our walk and our faith need to be like that. We need to have blinkers on like Bartimaeus and move forward. The very fact that Jesus said to him "what do you want me to do for you?", although he was obviously blind made me think that our prayers and what we ask for need to be very specific and we need to ask for exactly what we want. We need to speak it out and declare what we want in Jesus name as well.

Dee.C. Friend - London

INTRODUCTION

As you read through this account of the faith of 'Blind Bartimaeus', you will not only become an admirer of this man of outstanding courage, but you will be inspired to action as he was when you face what seems to be a 'hopeless situation'.

The story of 'Blind Bartimaeus' as told in the gospel of Mark, is an account of the extraordinary faith of a blind beggar who was about to be rewarded as Jesus of Nazareth, the long awaited Messiah, passed by.

So often when reading familiar Bible stories we see only the story as it is literally told but fail to receive the deep rich spiritual truths that God has prepared for us before the foundation of the world that will bless, encourage and enable us to receive godly wisdom to help us in our personal situations.

I invite you to meditate on the scriptures telling the Bartimaeus account and be strengthened by this unfolding drama which tells how a seemingly hopeless situation was dramatically turned around after an encounter with Jesus Christ. Through faith Bartimaeus was taken from the life of street beggar, to a joyful follower of Jesus, also having his name written into the Holy Bible.

Whilst writing this book around the year 2000, I was asked how much of Bartimaeus' story I personally identified with, and whether I was actually writing my own story, using Bartimaeus as the main character. In response to this I would say that I have surely had occasion to identify with some aspects of the life of Blind Bartimaeus as may many other people.

Ten people who watch the same film or listen to the same sermon, will each give a varied view, account or report of what they saw, heard or understood to be happening, and may even be able to identify aspects of their own life and character or that of others in it. The same is true of this story; you will at times be able to identify both yourself and others.

Blessed is the person who has never faced a seemingly hopeless situation. Courageous is the person who in the face of such a situation has expressed faith. However, to be forgiven is the person who we believe has attempted to discourage us from achieving our goal.

There are three things that I can assure you of today. The first is that God is real and is willing and able to intervene in the affairs of mankind.

The second is that God always responds to true faith. Those who truly believe and trust Him to make a difference in their circumstances will always be overcomers.

Thirdly, the situation of 'no hope', usually applies to those who do not or have not called on the name of the Lord Jesus Christ. To be without God or the knowledge of Him, is to have 'no hope'.

Faith in Jesus empowers us to see change in our situation and to receive the miracles that will bring it about. Faith in action enables us to overcome against all odds. It is faith in Jesus Christ that saves our souls.

As you read, please, enjoy, be encouraged and inspired to call upon the name of the Lord and receive your miracle. This book has been written with you in mind. God knew all about your struggle before you ever entered into it. He is willing and able to help you right now if you will just trust Him and put your life in His hands.

June Russell

UPDATE 2012

Since writing this book in the year 2000, I have faced and lived through some very great hardships like those outlined in this book. It is to the glory of God today that I have received the miracle of His restorative, resurrection power.

The Lord has given me 'beauty for ashes and the oil of joy for mourning.' I am a living testimony of how the God of 'all hope and comfort' takes the foolish and despised things of the world in order to confound the wise, so that no flesh may glory in His presence.

THE BARTIMAEUS ACCOUNT

This is the biblical account of the story of Blind Bartimaeus taken from the gospel of Mark chapter 10 verses 46-52:

46. Now they came to Jericho. As He (Jesus) went out of Jericho with His disciples and a great multitude, Blind Bartimaeus, the son of Timaeus, sat by the roadside begging.

47. And when he heard that it was Jesus of Nazareth, he began to cry out and say, "Jesus, Son of David, have mercy on me!"

48. Then many warned him to be quiet; but he cried out all the more, "Son of David, have mercy on me!"

49. So Jesus stood still and commanded him to be called. Then they called the blind man, saying to him, "Be of good cheer. Rise, He is calling you."

50. And throwing aside his garment, he rose and came to Jesus.

51. So Jesus answered and said to him, "What do you want Me to do for you?" The blind man said to Him, "Rabboni, that I may receive my sight."

52. Then Jesus said to him, "Go your way; your faith has made you well." And immediately he received his sight and followed Jesus on the road.

Additional accounts of the story of Blind Bartimaeus are told in Matthew 20:29-34 and Luke 18:35-43

Chapter 1

UPHOLDING THE FAMILY NAME

'Blind Bartimaeus' as he was called, was probably very well known in his community. It would not have been his outstanding contribution to society which made him well known, but the fact that he was blind. Bartimaeus, as a blind beggar sat by the roadside and called out for help each day over the years to the people as they passed him by.

One of the most interesting things about this blind man is the name that he was given. The name by which he had been called each day of his life up to the time when he met Jesus Christ face to face.

The recording of his name in the gospel of Mark (10:46) is Blind 'Bartimaeus', son of Timaeus.'

When it comes to upholding the family name, we will see that Bartimaeus really didn't have anything at all to be proud of. The New Testament Bible is translated from the Greek language which was widely spoken in those days. 'Bar' is a Greek word meaning 'Son of'; this was the first part of his name. 'Timaeus' is added to his name which makes him - Bar-Timaeus which all together reads 'Son of Timaeus'.

Most sons would be proud to have their father's name, but not this son; for the name 'Timaeus' means 'defiled or unclean.' It is apparent therefore, that Bartimaeus is not a man of noble birth.

According to the Hebrew customs of the Old Testament period, people who were born blind were mostly considered to be defiled or unclean.

Sin and disobedience under the law of the Hebrew people attracted various curses as their reward. **'The Lord will strike you with blindness and madness and confusion of heart'** (Deuteronomy 28:28). This was one of the penalties for sin mentioned in the Old Testament; however, we understand that since Jesus' resurrection, we are living in a period of grace whereby God has provided forgiveness of our sins and healing through the blood of Jesus.

To further understand the view which was commonly held, we can look at the account of another blind man who was healed by Jesus in the gospel of John 9:2,3, **'And His disciples** (Jesus') asked Him, saying **'Rabbi, who sinned, this man or his parents, that he was born blind?'** Jesus answered, **'Neither this man nor his parents sinned, but that the works of God should be revealed in him...'**

Therefore in the case of this particular blind man the cause of his blindness was not sin, but we can see that because he was blind the people assumed that he had sinned. The fact that this attitude was held, verifies the thought process of the people around 'Blind Bartimaeus.'

Rather than uphold the family name, Bartimaeus probably wanted to drop it. It was not only Bartimaeus that was born blind, but it appears his father also. The people probably assumed that it was what is known as a generational curse. A curse affecting another generation because of the sins of the father(s).

These curses are spoken of in Exodus 34:6-7. **'And the Lord passed before him** (Moses) **and proclaimed, "The lord, the Lord God, merciful and gracious, long-suffering, and abounding in goodness and truth, keeping mercy for thousands, forgiving iniquity and transgression and sin, by no means clearing the guilty, visiting the iniquity of the fathers upon the children and the children's children to the third and fourth generation."'**

The writer of the Psalms said: **'I have been young and I have been old, yet I have never seen the righteous forsaken, nor their descendants begging bread.'** (Psalm 37:25) The condition of Bartimaeus, who was both blind and a beggar, may have (rightly or wrongly) been evidence to the people of his community that either himself, or his family, were unrighteous or the perpetrators of sin.

Even though Bartimaeus himself was not the direct perpetrator of sin or iniquity, he was seemingly a bearer of its consequence, as was his father before him.

It is not uncommon that people suffer as a result of what their family has done. Having a bad name or reputation can hinder people from making progress in life when really it has nothing to do with them. The fact that you are related to somebody who has done something wrong can mean that you are 'guilty by association' in the eyes of others rather than because of anything that you have personally done. People can assume that because someone in your family has a bad name or reputation that the rest of the family will or have turned out that way.

Bartimaeus therefore really had no hope of a better future, for to all he was probably only ever going to be 'A blind beggar, born of a blind father whose family line had sinned.'

Apart from an inherited reputation there are of course people who through their own sins have a bad name or reputation that seems to follow them all through their life; some people are even proud of it because it gains them fear or false respect. Such things do not please God. God wants us all to be His children so that He can give us His name - Children of God (John 1:12). He wants us to be part of His family called 'holy and righteous.'

By reading Bartimaeus' story you'll see how through faith in Jesus Christ he was able to break the generational curse that seemed to be over his life, get rid of his bad name and rise above his current set of circumstances. Jesus Christ will do the same for you.

There are quite a few examples in the Bible where the Lord changed people's names. An example of this would be Jacob whose name meant 'deceiver'; however, when God changed this he was given the name 'Israel' meaning 'one who prevails with God.'

When the Lord dealt with Jacob's' bad reputation he then began to be a blessing to others. What God has done for others He can do for you too and give you the future and hope you so desire.

Chapter 2

THE LIFE OF BARTIMAEUS

For Bartimaeus, today was probably just like any other day. He'd probably resigned himself to the fact that he would spend another day begging by the roadside on the outskirts of Jericho. This was his livelihood, his occupation. This was Bartimaeus' way of life, begging and being dependent upon those who passed by for his very existence.

Bartimaeus made continuous, persistent requests for help with his life. He was probably troublesome and annoying to the people of his community. This would have been necessary because if he did not receive help from the people, Bartimaeus may have died in his state of poverty and lack.

It was not so in the days of the Old Testament, for God through Moses, had made provision for the poor to receive aid as part of the law. **'And you shall not glean your vineyard, nor shall you gather every grape of your vineyard; you shall leave them for the poor and the stranger...'** (Leviticus 19:10).

God is a merciful God as we learned in the scripture of Exodus 34:6. Despite the sins and subsequent condition of those who inherited curses, provision was still made for them. They were not ultimately forsaken, but in the New Testament era, there were increasingly more accounts of the poor and needy begging in order to survive. Such was the life of 'Blind Bartimaeus' on the streets of Jericho.

It was a seemingly hopeless situation that he was in. It must have been hard for Bartimaeus ever to have had anything to laugh about or to look forward to. Street life was his portion, sitting out each day in all weather conditions. It seemed there was no way out.

He could not even see a smiling face to encourage him. But what really must have hurt Bartimaeus, is that he did not bring this lifestyle upon himself. It was forced on him through circumstances and if that wasn't bad enough, people looked down on him because of his family name.

Bartimaeus had to get on with his life. Giving up was just not an option. To give up, or give in to the circumstances would probably have meant death. If he didn't beg, he didn't receive anything.

Bartimaeus must have longed for change but how could he go about it. He was trapped in a cycle of poverty and appeared to have no one who could help him out. But he was yet to meet the Master Way Maker, the One who makes a way when there seems to be no way.

There are times when we will feel trapped like 'Blind Bartimaeus'. We have reached a point where we can't go forward or backward. We just can't seem to find a way out of our circumstances and there is nobody around who can help us.

The suggestion will come to our minds that we should give up. After all, what have we got to live for? But to give up is dangerous. Giving up means that you may never reach your goal. You may never receive the blessing or breakthrough that is just around the corner if you would only hold on.

Giving up also means that we are denying the awesome power and willingness of God to turn our situation around. 'Faith' is the 'substance' that we must hold on to that will eventually bring about the thing which we cannot yet see but hope for.

Just because something is delayed it doesn't mean that it's never coming. Bartimaeus' story is evidence of that, even though he was suffering whilst waiting.

Romans 5: 3-5 says: '**...but we also glory in tribulations, knowing that tribulation produces perseverance; and perseverance character; and character hope. Now hope does not disappoint, because the love of God has been poured out in our hearts by the Holy Spirit who was given to us.**'

We are told here that tribulations bring perseverance which means that we have the ability to hold on during struggles. The perseverance changes and shapes our character. Through our renewed character we move from merely ‘holding on’ to ‘hoping ‘ which means we begin to be expectant about change.

As believers we are only able to do this because we have the Holy Spirit of God dwelling within our hearts.

For those who do not know Jesus Christ, there is no indwelling Holy Spirit and circumstances can seem to overwhelm them. In such cases people are often moved from hope to hopelessness.

Chapter 3

APPOINTMENT IN JERUSALEM

Jesus Christ was on His way to face the cross. He had entered and was now leaving Jericho, heading towards Jerusalem to lay down His life for all mankind. Jesus was fulfilling the prophetic word of Isaiah 50:7 which says: **'...Therefore I have set My face like flint...'.** The gospel of Luke records: **'He steadfastly set His face towards Jerusalem'** (9:51). Jesus knew that to go to Jerusalem would mean His death by crucifixion, but He was going in spite of this knowledge.

Jesus was on the road to divine destiny. His mind was focused on His mission, He was moving towards the goal that would bring eternal victory for all mankind and would grant for Him the upward call to His heavenly Father. Jesus Christ had come to give His life as a ransom for many (Mark 10:45), a living sacrifice. It was therefore with singleness of mind and a purposeful stride that He moved through Jericho that day. But was Jesus intending to stop along the way?

Jesus had been sent by His Father (God), to fulfil the promise given to Adam and Eve in the Garden of Eden after they had sinned and caused the fall of mankind thousands of years ago. He was the promised Saviour, the one through whom all of mankind could be restored to God and saved. He was on His way to conclude His mission which had begun with His incarnation and subsequent birth in a Bethlehem stable 33 years earlier.

This was the mission outlined prophetically in the Book of Isaiah 61:1-3: **'The Spirit of the Lord is upon Me; because the Lord has anointed Me to preach good tidings to the poor; he has sent Me to heal the broken-hearted, to proclaim liberty to the captives, and the opening of the prison door to those that are bound; To proclaim the acceptable year of the Lord, and the day of vengeance of our God; to comfort all that mourn; To console those who mourn in Zion, to give them beauty for ashes, the oil of joy for mourning, the garment of praise for the spirit of heaviness; that they might be called trees of righteousness, the**

planting of the Lord that He may be glorified.'

Throughout scripture we see statements of purpose and intent pertaining to the earthly mission and ministry of Jesus. He said: '**...I have come that they might have life and that they might have it more abundantly...**', (John 10:10b) and in another place it is stated that '**...for this purpose the Son of God was manifested, that He might destroy the works of the devil...**' (1 John 3:8)

In the Bible book of Acts the Apostle Paul confirms Jesus' ministry '**...God anointed Jesus of Nazareth with the Holy Spirit and with power, who went about doing good and healing all who were oppressed by the devil...**' (Acts 10:38).

Now this final part of Jesus' mission was to sacrifice His own life so that His blood could pay the price for the sins of the whole world before God. '**For God so loved the world that He gave His only begotten Son that whosoever should believe in Him would not perish but have everlasting life**' (John 3:16).

This would make a way for mankind to again have the living personal relationship with God that He'd intended; the relationship which was ruined by the sins of Adam and Eve (when they were deceived by the devil) - the first of Gods created people. These sins caused mankind to be separated from God but God's response to this situation was to lovingly accept the blood of His own Son as a sacrifice for the sins of the world. '**But God demonstrates His own love toward us, in that while we were still sinners, Christ died for us**' Romans 5:8.

Chapter 4

THE MULTITUDE

Jesus Christ is the Word of God (John 1:1-4), and everywhere the Word (Jesus) went, signs and wonders followed. But it wasn't only signs and wonders that followed Jesus, but people also, and on this occasion they are described as 'a great multitude.' There is no record in the Bible of how many people constitutes 'a multitude', but we know that on one occasion when Jesus fed more than five thousand people, they were called a multitude.

This group of followers was 'a great multitude' so we can guess that there were more than five thousand people with Him that day.

Religious groups often followed Jesus too; they were astonished by His knowledge of scripture and His authority. These were called the Sanhedrin, the Pharisees and the Sadducees, but most of this entire multitude was made up of 'the common people'. Every day people including tax collectors, beggars, lepers (at a distance), prostitutes, the poor, the sick, the disabled, the ethnic minorities, and the needy, in fact the very people with whom He spent most of His time.

Amongst others there were the neglected, rejected, the despised and outcast, the down-trodden and broken. Those who once had no future and no hope. Yes, they were probably all there that day. The common people. Ordinary everyday people.

There were women, children, farmers and fishermen, all banded together like a great army that marched through the streets of Jericho.

An army of people, the like of which may not have been seen in Jericho since the days that the children of Israel had marched around its walls thousands of years ago.

These were the people who followed Him, supported Him and wanted to be around Him every place He went. You see these people knew that Jesus was genuine. He had given them something lasting, something true and He always delivered what He had promised. Jesus gave the people direction for their lives and He accepted them regardless of who and what they were. Jesus Christ made a difference in the life of the common people. What He had was for all mankind, but it was the common people who readily accepted it, (Mark 12:37).

Many times in my life I have been in or around a crowd of people. Every one of them seems to have the same goal or objective. They all seem to know where they are going but somehow, even though I was one of them, I just didn't feel part of them.

I felt as though I was an onlooker, I was bewildered and unable to join the crowd. Circumstances in my life would not allow me to go or to keep up with them and I was stuck where I was in my situation. The amazing thing was that nobody seemed to notice me or my situation and this left me feeling even more isolated. Often as 'Blind Bartimaeus' was about to find out, you have the feeling of being passed by.

We cannot always go with the crowd, nor will the crowd always recognize what is going on in our lives that may prevent us from going with them. As a believer in Christ we are not to become detached from them since in Christ there is one body of people. We must however seek an encounter with Christ that will enable our circumstances to be changed in order that we can fully function as a member of the body of Christ.

If you are not a believer or follower of Christ and His ways it may be that you no longer feel comfortable following the usual crowd and that God is calling you into relationship with Him and to be amongst His people.

Whatever the situation may be, there is an answer and as we will go on to see with 'Blind Bartimaeus' that answer will always be and can only be found in Jesus Christ.

Chapter 5

THE CRY FOR HELP

When Jesus passed by that day with His great multitude of followers, He passed right by Blind Bartimaeus as he sat by the roadside begging. Of course Bartimaeus wanted to know right away what was happening, and he was told that Jesus of Nazareth was passing by.

Mark 10:47 begins, **'and when he heard that it was Jesus of Nazareth...'** These words show that Bartimaeus heard something that moved him to action. The Bible says that, **'Faith comes by hearing and hearing by the word of God'** (Romans 10:17). There was something about the name of Jesus that spoke deeply to him and he quickly associated Jesus with his deliverance, healing and wholeness. He began to call on His name, **'Jesus, Son of David, have mercy on me'** (Mark 10:47). Faith arose in the heart of 'Blind Bartimaeus'.

By calling Him 'Son of David', Bartimaeus was acknowledging Jesus' royal bloodline and family ties. It was an affirmation, that this man would be king of an eternal throne, a throne which would never diminish or end as promised to King David in the Old Testament prophecy, (2 Samuel 7:12-13,16).

Bartimaeus knew that if he could just get Jesus' attention, get into His presence, he would receive a miracle. Bartimaeus had a need, a need that was great. He was a desperate man.

It is not known how old he was or how long he'd been sitting on the streets and on the fringes of society, dependent upon his community for his daily bread. Nobody knew how bad he felt, or how much he had suffered because of his name and blindness that he'd had held since birth.

However long Bartimaeus had been looking to others to help him live his life, he had never received anything from them that would lift him above his circumstances, take him off the streets or give him lasting peace. He had never received anything that made a difference to him or bound up the wounds of his hidden, broken heart. But today Jesus of Nazareth was passing by, and if he could only make himself heard, get Jesus' attention, things need never be the same again, for of the Lord it is said: **'He heals the broken-hearted and binds up their wounds'** (Psalm 147:3).

He had probably heard all about Jesus and how He went around doing good; about how the deaf could hear, the lame could walk, lepers were cleansed, the dead were raised, demons cast out and the blind people were made to see after their encounter with Jesus. Bartimaeus needed such an encounter and he intended getting this need met today. Bartimaeus lifted his voice and cried out for mercy.

Bartimaeus gave a cry from the heart. It was the heart of a man who was probably wounded, scorned by his community because of his family history, his name and his blindness, a man broken by the depth of his desperate situation and suffering, a man who realised that he may never get this close to Jesus again, and he never would have, because Jesus wasn't coming back that way... at least not to minister in the way that he had been doing.

Jesus wasn't stopping...He was on His way to a much higher call..., the sacrifice of His own life which meant that in the future He would be able to touch the lives of all men everywhere through the Holy Spirit of God. So this man, 'Blind Bartimaeus' wasn't going to let Jesus pass him by... he needed a touch from Him right here, right now.

You see, Bartimaeus was never going to meet Jesus by a well like the Samaritan woman; he wasn't able to come to Him like the leper or fight his way through the crowd like the woman with the issue of blood.

Jesus didn't notice him and stop as He did with the blind man in John chapter nine, or come to his house like with Zacchaeus. He wasn't being brought to Him like so many others had been, and he had no faithful friends to bring him on a stretcher as the man whose friends had lowered him through the roof. No, this man had nothing but 'blind faith' to get Jesus' attention that day, so when he cried out, he cried out with all of his heart, through pain, fears, frustration and desperation, and with all of his feelings of hopelessness.

The moment that Bartimaeus began to call out, his heart must have been pounding in his chest; maybe tears were rolling down his face as he pleaded for attention from Jesus. At all costs, Bartimaeus had to get to Jesus that day.

Chapter 6

FAITH THROUGH SUFFERING

Bartimaeus was in no doubt about what Jesus could do for him and though he had suffered all of his life, his suffering had not destroyed his ability to believe, trust and have faith in the Son of God. He knew about the coming Messiah - 'The Anointed Son of God'.

Bartimaeus had confidence that Jesus Christ was the answer to all of his problems. Maybe he had heard the scripture from the book of Isaiah, which said: **'Then the eyes of the blind shall be opened, the ears of the deaf shall be unstopped. Then the lame shall leap like a deer, and the tongue of the dumb shall sing. For waters shall burst forth in the wilderness, and streams in the desert,'** (Isaiah 35:5-6).

Bartimaeus' faith left no doubt that he would receive something from Jesus Christ. He was expectant that an audience with Jesus would solve all of his problems. In fact, so great was this man's faith, that he could identify with the Psalmist who said: **'I would have lost heart, unless I had believed that I would see the goodness of the Lord in the land of the living'** (Psalm 27:13) for if anybody at all had a reason to lose heart... it was 'Blind Bartimaeus' but he did not.

Throughout his time of suffering Bartimaeus had not lost his faith. He was discouraged at times, yes, he got weary, and he often felt helpless, yes - but he had not given up. He believed that Jesus Christ could and would make a difference in his life and his belief did not allow him to go under or to be overwhelmed by the greatness of his problems.

When we struggle in life against great trials, when we battle on against great odds we must set our face like flint as Jesus did and be determined that we will overcome them all in His name.

The Bible tells believers that though our faith is tested and tried that we will be rewarded when we endure and also that God will never allow us to suffer beyond what we are able to endure. There is often much suffering before glory but when we come out the other side it makes the victory even sweeter, and we are made stronger.

Jesus Christ won the ultimate victory following His death and resurrection for all of mankind. When we know and understand this we realise that in Jesus we can do all things and that there is no battle we fight for which the victory has not already been won.

There is really no need for anybody to be in a hopeless situation because Jesus died so that we could all have abundant life through Him. We find that when we come to Jesus and cast all of our cares upon Him we will receive the peace and faith to overcome in times of suffering, tribulations, and great trials.

Chapter 7

THE SPIRITUALLY BLIND

Earlier it was said that those who knew or saw Bartimaeus may have held a certain unfavourable opinion about him. However, it was not just this group of people but seemingly most of the community. The scripture says 'many'. This word 'many' in Greek actually means 'multitude.'

So there was a multitude of people who were against him getting to Jesus. It must have been a terrifying experience for a blind man to be faced with such a mountain of opposition. When we read further in that passage of scripture it says that as Bartimaeus called out to Jesus...**they sternly warned him to be quiet** (Mark 10:48). In actual fact these people were threatening Bartimaeus.

These people lacked spiritual insight and seemingly had no perspective about the matters of which Jesus always taught. Their hearts were yet to be enlightened to the fact that Jesus' ministry was based on meeting the needs of the people through the power of His love. He delighted in touching the lives of people such as this in order that God would be glorified. Jesus loves people.

So the people warned Bartimaeus to be quiet. 'Don't ask Jesus to help you' is basically what they were saying...'Jesus is busy. Jesus has an appointment in Jerusalem and He cannot stop for you. Who are you to call to Jesus...Don't you know that you are a blind beggar, the son of an unclean and defiled blind man? Jesus can't stop for you because you're just not important enough.' 'Stay in your place', this is the message that some of these people were giving to Bartimaeus, even if they were not saying it directly. But the message that they were giving was not the 'good tidings of great joy' that Jesus had come to preach. This was not the gospel. Their words gave Bartimaeus no joy, no hope, no comfort, no encouragement.

These people did not just tell Bartimaeus to be quiet, they actually 'sternly warned' him. They tried to intimidate him, to stop him from calling out to the Son of God. A warning generally means that there will be a consequence for the person if they do not take notice. A warning ignored is usually followed by some type of action which is unfavourable towards the person being warned.

The reaction of the people evidently shows that some of those followers of Christ and of His word needed to become more like Him because they were giving a wrong testimony or representation of Christ.

'But the natural man does not receive the things of the spirit of God, for they are foolishness to him; nor can he know them because they are spiritually discerned.' (1 Corinthians 2:14)

It was mostly because of the Jewish laws and customs that the people would have tried to prevent Bartimaeus from reaching Jesus. An unclean or defiled person was not allowed to have association with or touch a Rabbi or priest. This was to prevent them from becoming tainted or defiled by the sin or disease of the person who was approaching them. This line of Jewish thinking would therefore hinder them from expressing love and compassion towards those who desperately sought help and relief from their situation.

Chapter 8

THE COURAGE OF BARTIMAEUS

Bartimaeus the blind beggar from Jericho was a man who was expressing great faith. He was calling on the name of the Lord. 'Jesus, Son of David, have mercy on me.' He had heard the people around him with their threats and intimidation, but he was not about to be stopped.

Bartimaeus wanted something from Jesus and it is reported that he ignored the threats, gained courage and called out all the more (Mark 10:48).

Bartimaeus truly wanted the righteousness which could only come from an encounter with Jesus Christ; but as he pursued it the people turned on him and presented themselves as an obstacle.

The people, as many as there were would have towered over Bartimaeus as he sat by the roadside. They didn't seem to respect him and probably thought that they were better than he was.

He wanted the touch of the Lord upon his life that would dramatically turn his circumstances around. He was persistent in his crying out because he hungered for it. His persistent faith however, would soon make him the recipient of the kingdom of heaven. This made Bartimaeus all the more determined to get to Jesus and he doubled his efforts in calling out. The prize was going to be worth all of the effort.

No amount of persecution, threats or dissuasion was going to stop Bartimaeus today. All fear left Bartimaeus, he became extremely bold and courageous and he took a giant leap of faith over all of the human obstacles and hurdles in his way.

Here we see the first of his miracles that day. You may recall that a great multitude was following Jesus at this time, maybe as many as ten or fifteen thousand people or more. Imagine the sound of thousands of feet, young and old, fast and slow, all pursuing the Lord Jesus Christ. In addition to this, voices, shouts, cries and excited chatter, but above all of these Bartimaeus made his voice heard.

Perhaps it was the years of begging that had fine-tuned his vocal cords to project his voice in such a way that he would be heard over a multitude; but Bartimaeus made himself heard that day. He wasn't going to allow himself to be bullied into silence, and he wasn't going to be put off by the fact that countless others were blocking the way to the Lord Jesus.

Bartimaeus used what he had, 'the cry for help', an art that he had perfected over the many years that he had been begging on the streets and he cried out in an exceedingly loud voice **'Son of David have mercy on me.'**

When 'blind faith' is all you have left - use it - you will get what you need from God. Don't look at the faces of those who discourage you. Look into the face of the Son of God. Understand that only He can truly give you both what you want and what you need.

Often our greatest fears can be of people. We see them as 'giants in the land' as the children of Israel did at the borders of the Promised Land. Friend, God is bigger than people and He is bigger than our problems. There is nothing too difficult for Him to do.

Remember this one thing: If you focus on the obstacles in your way you will tell yourself that your problems are too great, but if you focus on Jesus you will say - I cannot, but He can, "for what is impossible with man is possible with God. For with God nothing shall be impossible," (Mark 10:27).

Jesus can see the way out of your circumstance since this was the reason for which He came. Trust Him wholeheartedly and launch out in 'blind faith'.

Chapter 9

LOVE TO MEET HIS NEED

Mercy is what Bartimaeus sought. It was the cry of his heart '...have mercy on me...' What is mercy? The Hebrew word for mercy is 'Hesed' which is 'kindness'. The Greek word depicting the mercy that Bartimaeus required is 'Eleeo' which is 'sympathy manifested in an act' or 'to have pity on'. Another Greek variation of 'mercy' is 'Eleos' which is compassion.

Mercy is basically a form or type of love. This is what Bartimaeus was asking for. The type or measure of love given is determined by the state or condition of its intended recipient. The state could be one of suffering and need, while the one calling for it might be unworthy or ill-deserving. Such was the case of Bartimaeus in the eyes of the people.

Mercy is the disposition of love after being aware of all the relevant facts, and the kindly ministry of love for the person's relief. It is a Christian grace.

'...God who is rich in mercy, because of His great love with which He loved us...'(Ephesians 2:4.) God is the giver of mercy, and His solution to the problem of a sinful world separated from Him is the evidence of such mercy. **'But God demonstrates His own love towards us, in that while we were still sinners, Christ died for us' (**Romans 5:8.) God showed an outward manifestation of pity and provided resources adequate to meet the need of Him who showed it (Jesus). Jesus by showing mercy would now become the benefactor of Bartimaeus.

In the Bible book of Hebrews we see encouragement to come to God for mercy for all our needs. **'Let us therefore come boldly to the throne of grace that we may obtain mercy and find grace to help in time of need'** (Hebrews 4:16). This grace of 'mercy' is what Bartimaeus asked for, that Jesus would show him the form of love that would end his misery and meet his need.

So Bartimaeus was not giving in and he wasn't giving up. He had heard enough about Jesus' earthly ministry, and his knowledge of prophecy concerning the Messiah, Son of God, would most certainly have convinced him that '...**without faith it is impossible to please Him, for he who comes to God must believe that He is and that He is a rewarder of those who DILIGENTLY seek Him**' (Hebrews 11:6).

Every day Bartimaeus' cup would be filled with the offerings of pity, goodwill, loose change and scorn; but today only mercy would be good enough for him. He must have been tired of scraping by, being ignored, knocked about, walked over, talked about and sneered at. He was tired of the ache and emptiness in his heart, the loneliness and separation from even the common people.

He was probably tired of suppressing his dreams of a better life because... well, it just never seemed possible and to dream was to hurt and to re-open wounds that were 'oh so deep' and never seemed to heal. Bartimaeus was tired of being blind.

Today Bartimaeus wanted his cup to overflow with the joy of having his needs met by the Lord Jesus Christ; mercy applied to his situation like balm that would heal the wounds of yesteryear and bring him peace for all his tomorrows. Oh, how he must have longed to say along with David the Psalmist, '**Surely goodness and mercy shall follow me all the days of my life; and I shall dwell in the house of the Lord forever**' (Psalm 23:6).

Chapter 10

GETTING JESUS' ATTENTION

So it was that Bartimaeus got Jesus' attention that day; for it is reported that '...**Jesus stood still**...' (Mark 10:49). As mentioned before, there was a great bustling multitude of people on the move before him; but Bartimaeus succeeded in making his voice heard. Maybe he had heard about the parable of the persistent widow, where Jesus said '...**Men always ought to pray and not lose heart**' (Luke 18:1).

Yes, at last Bartimaeus' prayer and cries had been heard and Jesus Christ, the Son of God, stood still and 'commanded' him to be called. He 'commanded'. This word 'commanded' means that Jesus gave strict instruction, He gave an order.

The authority with which He commanded was the same type of authority that He used when he called the man Lazarus out of the tomb alive after being dead for four days. Therefore, all those who had previously sought to prevent Bartimaeus from reaching the Lord were now in no doubt that Jesus was going to respond to his need. These same people were now instructed to bring Bartimaeus into the Lord's presence.

Yes, Jesus had a lot on His mind that day, the destiny of the world lay upon His shoulders as He went to face the cross. Yet, Jesus stopped at Bartimaeus' cries. He laid aside His own burden to meet the needs of another.

Now the people would see that Bartimaeus was important to Jesus, for He did not view Blind Bartimaeus in the same way as they did. He was not looking through the eyes of man, but through the loving eyes of a merciful God.

Jesus was not concerned about his history, heritage, name, occupation or reputation; no, Jesus was responding to the true cry from the heart, He was responding to this man's faith in His ability to fulfil his need.

Jesus Christ was the champion of the poor and needy, and now His divine love and power was about to be applied to the situation of Blind Bartimaeus; aiding him in his life-long struggle and giving him the victory over his circumstances.

'Now thanks be to God who always leads us in triumph in Christ, and through us diffuses the fragrance of His knowledge in every place' (1 Corinthians 2:14).

When Jesus stopped to help Bartimaeus all of the people suddenly became aware that He is interested in those people which others consider to be untouchables or outcasts and this is how the knowledge of His goodness and grace spreads.

Chapter 11

CHANGE IN ATTITUDE

Peoples' attitudes can dramatically change when they realize that the thoughts of the leader or somebody else that they hold in high esteem are different from theirs. At the beginning of Jesus' earthly ministry He would not receive the adulation and praise of the people around Him, for He said that He knew the hearts of all men, signifying that peoples' hearts could change from praise to criticism at any time.

There was a time when the people would shout for Him to be king - in fact that very same crowd that now accompanied Him to Jerusalem; but only a few short days later they would not shout 'crown Him, crown Him' but 'crucify Him, crucify Him' at the encouragement of the religious leaders of the day.

Jesus was not swayed by the people's opinion of Blind Bartimaeus or any other 'outcast' of society. He loved them with a deep and compassionate love that went way beyond the surface. It went all the way to the cross.

Jesus spent most of His time with them, and He knew that it was the effect of sin in their lives that had wounded and corrupted people and led them to their current day circumstances and situations.

Jesus could see far beyond the here and now - He knew the end of a situation from the beginning, and He could see the result of a man or a woman whose life is touched by the finger of a merciful and compassionate God.

He had seen repeatedly that His mission of setting captives free made a difference in peoples' lives; that when they met with the true and living God they were dramatically transformed into the people that God had created and intended them to be.

So Jesus gave Bartimaeus the time and attention He needed, and in an instant the attitude of those around Bartimaeus changed, and so did their behaviour towards him,... **for 'If God was for him, who could be against him'** (Romans 8:31). **'Be of good cheer'** they now said, **'Rise, He is calling you.'** To be of good cheer meant to have courage and confidence. This came from the very same people, who a few short minutes ago had warned him to be quiet. They now had a change of heart when they saw he was worthy of Jesus' attention. He now became a 'somebody' in their eyes. Yes, **'Rise'** he was told by those who had previously kept him down; **'Be of good cheer'** he was told by those who had just threatened him - **'HE IS CALLING...YOU!'**

Jesus Christ of Nazareth had stopped, stood still and commanded the man to be 'called', but now it was Bartimaeus' turn to step out in the faith that he had and approach the Lord. **'For without faith it is impossible to please Him'** (Hebrews 11:6).

Chapter 12

THROWING HINDRANCES ASIDE

Bartimaeus did not have to be persuaded any further to go to Jesus. He did not need to be told a second time. The first thing he did was to throw aside his garment. Now this was an interesting action. What did that garment symbolise to Bartimaeus, that he should cast it aside so readily?

Maybe it was a beggar's coat - something that signified to others that he was poor, needy and blind. Maybe to him it was his only comfort as he wallowed in the depths of self-pity at the roadside in Jericho. Whatever it was, it was an outer covering which hid the true person, and what was going on inside of his heart.

In Old Testament scripture, a garment was often used symbolically of either evil or righteous covering. Maybe this garment was yet another thing by which people judged who and what he was. It is the characteristic of man to look upon the outside and to make a judgement, summary or assumption about a person, but not so with God.

The Bible tells us that when the Prophet Samuel was looking at all Jesse's sons to find the one who should be anointed king, God told him', **'Do not look at his appearance or at his physical stature..., For the Lord does not see as man sees; for man looks at the outward appearance, but God looks at the heart.'** (1 Samuel 16:7).

What was Bartimaeus' action indicative of that day? His garment by which he was recognized, was probably encrusted with the filth of living every day on the edge of society. Caked with layers of self-pity, grief, rejection and self-protection, a blind beggar's coat. This garment may have been a reminder of who he was, and of his background, and everything else that had led to his miserable existence for many years. But Bartimaeus didn't need this anymore, he was about to receive the garment of praise (Isaiah 61:3).

So it was with great emphasis that he threw aside this symbol of hindrance, heartache and unrighteousness, and in faith he rose and went to Jesus in the sight of all the people. He was putting his faith into action.

Now that he had been 'called', he wasn't going to let anything hinder him anymore. He was not going to trip over that garment. No, he didn't need that covering anymore. So he threw it off, and the very moment that this garment was off his back, Bartimaeus arose and came into the presence of the Lord.

'Therefore..., since we are surrounded by so great a cloud of witnesses, let us lay aside every weight and the sin which so easily ensnares us...' (Hebrews 12:1).

Chapter 13

ASK AND YOU SHALL RECEIVE

When Bartimaeus came before Jesus, he was asked **'What do you want me to do for you?'** (Mark 10:51a). Jesus was there and willing to listen, He knew that Bartimaeus had asked Him for mercy - undeserved relief from his circumstances in the eyes of the people; but He wanted Bartimaeus to be specific about his need. Jesus had sufficient grace (undeserved favour) to meet every need.

God is rich in mercy, and therefore, there was is abundant supply of His grace. With God there is no lack, and there is nothing too difficult for Him to do. It was not that Jesus could not see that this man was blind, but rather that he wanted him to extend his faith and request specifically what he believed the Lord could do for him. When Jesus gave him his request in the sight of the people, it would encourage everyone to approach the Lord in faith.

'Ask', says the Lord **'and it will be given to you; seek and you will find; knock, and it will be opened to you. For everyone who asks receives, and he who seeks finds, and to him who knocks it shall be opened.'** (Matthew 7:7-8).

Jesus had everything that this man needed and He was prepared to give it to him. **'No good thing would the Lord withhold from him.'** (Psalm 84:11) If he asked for bread, he wasn't going to get a stone.

The apostle John encourages us to ask of the Lord by saying: **'Now this is the confidence that we have in Him, that if we ask anything according to His will, He hears us. And if we know that He hears us, whatever we ask, we know that we have the petitions that we have asked of Him.'** (1 John 5: 14-15).

As we read through the Bible, we see many times how the Lord encourages us to come to him for the things we need. It is God's desire to help us and to meet our needs. He wants us to be dependent on Him. He wants us to come like children to their father. He has given us many examples in the Bible of how we should ask things from Him:

- **Ask in faith without doubting** (James 1:6)
- **Ask according to His will** (1 John 5:14-15)
- **Ask in Jesus' name** (John 14:14)
- **Be persistent** (Luke 18:1)
- **Be specific**(Mark 10:51a/Matthew 6:7)

Understanding that it is the will of God to help us, and asking in faith are two important steps to receiving from God. Reading the Bible gives us a clearer understanding of what the will of God is.

Chapter 14

BARTIMAEUS PRAYER IS ANSWERED

Bartimaeus had understanding of what the will of God was and knowing the purpose of Jesus' mission, asked in faith, '**...that I may receive my sight.**' (Mark 10:51b). This was something that he wasn't able to ask of any other person. In all his days there was never anybody who had given Bartimaeus the thing which he desired most of all. None of the 'religious leaders' were able, but God was able, that day and every day **'For with God, nothing shall be impossible'** (Luke 1:37).

Bartimaeus did not ask for riches which would keep him all of his days. He wasn't looking for a hand-out. He didn't want to be a dependent in society. He didn't ask Jesus to change his name or give him good standing in the community. Bartimaeus wanted to receive his sight. He wanted to see where he was going. It was something that he'd never had, but it was something that he'd hoped for.

He wanted the scriptures and prophesies to be fulfilled in his life, this day. He believed, he had held on to the word of God in his heart, and therefore now was his moment of truth, so to speak. For the word of God says: **'And you shall know the truth and the truth shall set you free'** (John 8:32).

The truth, that the coming Messiah could and would open the eyes of the blind, was a truth that Bartimaeus could cherish. This would have compelled him to call upon the name of the Lord and it was about to become a living reality in his life. He had not called in vain, for the Word of God which is living and active was about to cause an effect in his life, right here and now. He would come out of physical darkness for the first time in his life and find himself standing before Jesus Christ, 'The Light and Hope of the world.'

Chapter 15

HIS TRANSFORMING PRESENCE

In the United Kingdom in the 1990's there was a series of advertisements on national television about one-to-one mobile phones. There was always the same question, 'Who would you like to have a one-to-one with?' Various people would name their heroes whether dead or alive and imagine what it would be like to have a face-to-face talk with them.

Bartimaeus was in this position and the person he most wanted a one-to-one with was Jesus Christ. Being in His presence meant everything to him. In this particular account the Bible does not state whether Jesus touched Bartimaeus or how exactly his healing and deliverance came about; but what we do know is that after just a few moments in the presence of the Lord Bartimaeus was a transformed man.

He was now a man with a vision where before he had none. He came out with far more than he had asked Jesus for. How it was done we do not know, but what we know for sure is that from His presence there came fullness of joy. Bartimaeus had a one-to-one with Jesus Christ and was a new man. All of the problems that were associated with this man for so many years disappeared in an instant. They just fell away because of a brief encounter in the presence of the Lord Jesus Christ.

These were the second and third miracles which Bartimaeus experienced that day. The first was that he was able to make himself heard over the multitude, the second was that he was able to approach Jesus since Jewish law did not allow defiled people to come near priests or 'religious leaders'. Jesus broke all of these restrictive traditions when He commanded Bartimaeus to be brought to Him.

The third miracle was, of course the one of Bartimaeus receiving his sight. Having been in this condition from birth he experienced a supernatural occurrence which cannot be explained.

Jesus' ministry was full of signs and wonders which demonstrated to the people that God was sovereign and at work in the affairs of men and through miracles such as this, many believed and became followers.

Chapter 16

IT WAS FAITH - NOT OPPORTUNITY

Faith moves the hand of God - it really does please Him, and as the writer of Hebrews said: '...**he who comes to God must believe that He is, and that He is a rewarder of those who diligently seek Him'** (Hebrews 11:6b)

It is not the fact that Bartimaeus had the opportunity to get to Jesus Christ, because really it was no opportunity at all. All the odds were stacked against him getting there. It was Bartimaeus' faith that was the vehicle that drove him to the Lord. It was his faith that Jesus commented on when He said '...**Go your way; your faith has made you well'** (Mark 10:52a).

Bartimaeus may well have had the opportunity to come before Jesus, but he may not have had the faith to receive a miracle. The gospel of Matthew, chapter 13 verse 58 tells us that when Jesus was in His home town (Nazareth) even though many people had the opportunity to be before Him, He couldn't do many miracles there because of their unbelief.

Opportunity does not constitute faith and a miracle is never the outcome of the opportunity to receive from God. A miracle is the outcome of the faith which is necessary to believe and receive it, just as Blind Bartimaeus did. It was his faith in Jesus Christ, the Son of God, that led him to receive his sight that day, and his faith changed the course of his destiny forever. His faith was the substance of something he'd hoped for, the evidence of something yet unseen, which allowed his whole being to be touched by God. It was his faith that opened his blind eyes.

This man's determination to receive what he believed only Jesus Christ could give him, secured his immediate and permanent healing. His ability to overcome obstacles, hindrances and seemingly impossible circumstances, meant that he, 'Bartimaeus' - blind beggar man of an unclean, blind father from Jericho, neglected, rejected and dejected, hopeless, helpless, outcast of society... was written into the scriptures, The Holy Bible, The Word of God.

He is an everlasting example to all generations of how faith and a supernatural encounter with Jesus Christ lifts you above your circumstances, causes you to throw off and leave behind all hindrances, and receive a brand new life in Jesus Christ.

Chapter 17

THE WAY - THE TRUTH - THE LIFE

When Jesus Christ miraculously gave Bartimaeus sight, he told him **'...Go your way...'** (Mark 10:52a). Jesus had given him the precious gift that he sought, but He didn't demand that he now follow Him. That's just not Jesus' way. Jesus gives an open invitation for people to come to Him, know Him personally and receive all the love and blessings of that relationship. But Jesus never forced anybody to follow Him.

He said to Bartimaeus, **'go your way'.** But Bartimaeus was not like the nine forgetful and ungrateful l lepers of Luke 17:11-19. He was thankful and did not forget the mercy that Jesus had shown him.

He wanted to be around Jesus. To be with the Man who had given him the abundant life that he was now beginning to experience. Now that his eyes had opened, he saw the living truth of God's word before his very eyes. And what a sight it must have been for him to meet his Lord and Saviour face to face. What joy now flooded his soul.

Bartimaeus was now a living testimony of the manifested grace, love, mercy and power of God through Jesus Christ. He must have been so glad because his mourning had been turned into dancing. He must have been so glad that he never gave up hoping for a better life which he had now found, thanks to Jesus. He probably could not contain his joy and wanted to tell everybody what had happened to him, and to encourage them to go to Jesus because He really is the only One with all the answers for your life today.

Yes, I think that Bartimaeus must have shouted up and down the streets of Jericho that day: **'Oh, I would have lost heart; unless I had believed that I would see the goodness of the Lord in the land of the living'** (Psalm 27:13).

Now that he had received this goodness and mercy, he wasn't going to take what he had received and go his own way. Goodness and mercy were to follow him all the days of his life. He knew the truth and the truth had set him free. So now he was going to go the way of Jesus. For Jesus is **'...the way, the truth and the life'** (John 14:6) and this is what Bartimaeus wanted. After all, why should he go away from Jesus now?

Why should he go back to the people who had never encouraged him or helped him a great deal, people who could never give him that which he needed and desired most? Why should he go back to his old lifestyle that had caused him so much pain, when he had received so much love and blessing from Jesus?

Jesus cares about the whole person, not just one aspect of their life. Jesus heals from the roots up; he doesn't just put a plaster on a wound.

Because of Jesus, Bartimaeus' whole life changed. The generational curse of blindness and poverty was broken and Bartimaeus could now live a full and joy-filled life. He could go where he wanted and do what he wanted, even get a new occupation. His future was secured, because he had believed in Jesus Christ the Son of God. Now Bartimaeus was able to share in spreading the 'good tidings of great joy,' because he had a true message of hope for all people who were in his former situation.

There was nothing that could compare to knowing Jesus. Everything else just paled into insignificance. It was because of Jesus that he now had his sight, a future and a hope, and because of Jesus that he would now continue to walk in faith after the Son of God - Jesus Christ the Son of David who had mercy on him.

And so for Bartimaeus, who once sat by the roadside begging, it was no longer 'business as usual.' He now walked upon that road. He joined the 'great multitude,' for he had decided to follow Jesus.

Joining the multitude meant that Bartimaeus was amongst many of the people who tried to prevent him from reaching the Lord. Did he hold a grudge? Not Bartimaeus, he was completely transformed.

Now Bartimaeus had received his physical sight, he wasn't using it in this walk after Jesus. No, this was a walk of faith, trusting in the

Lord Jesus Christ that he would continually lead him in the paths of righteousness, fully believing that **'The steps of a righteous man are ordered by the Lord...'** (Psalm 37:23).

THE GOSPEL MESSAGE

Jesus Christ, The Son of God, came to earth, lived and died on a cross so that each person would have the opportunity to come to God through Him. This means that God punished Jesus for our sins and for all who now believe in Jesus there is forgiveness of sins.

Jesus is the hope of the world and the hope of the hopeless and therefore you have no reason to despair. He is and has the answer.

A blind man saw the truth, but he was only able to overcome through meeting Jesus Christ. When Jesus saw the blind man, He saw potential. Jesus came to his rescue and gave him a brand new life. A New Beginning.

Although we may not see Jesus in the flesh today, we know that He is alive because He rose from the dead.

Jesus says that whoever comes to Him He will never turn away. He says: **'I am the way, the truth and the life'.** He says, 'Come **to Me all you who are weary and heavy laden, and I will give you rest for your weary souls'.**

This is a life changing message. An Eternal Message. The Bible says that **'whoever calls upon the name of the Lord shall be saved'** (Romans 10:13). If you want to accept Jesus' invitation to eternal life and forgiveness of sins, you can say the following prayer with all of your heart.

SALVATION PRAYER

Dear Lord Jesus,

I believe that you are the Son of God and that you died on the cross for all of my sins. I thank you for loving me enough to die for me.

I know that I am sinful and separated from God and that I need your forgiveness and a personal relationship with you.

I now turn away from my sins, and ask for your forgiveness and that you would come into my heart and life and take over. I give myself totally to you and want you to lead and guide my life and teach me all of your ways.

Please give me a new heart and a new spirit and never let me turn back from following you.

Thank you for hearing my prayer.
In Jesus name. Amen.

If you have truly prayed this prayer from your heart you are now a child of God and have been born-again of His spirit. You are a new creation in Jesus Christ; you are saved.

Ask God to lead you to a Bible believing and practising church where you can meet other believers and grow in the knowledge of Him.

CONTACT DETAILS

This book comes to you with blessing. If you have been blessed reading it or would like to share something relevant then please contact:

June Russell

Email: jrussell@lifeinthekingdom.co.uk
or write to:

June Russell
Life in the Kingdom
PO Box 66289
London
SW6 9FE

OTHER TITLES AVAILABLE

- If it's good enough for Jesus…it's good enough for you!
- No hard cases - The story of a Christian Psychiatric Nurse
- House of Grace
- Watch and Pray
- You can do it…in Jesus name!
- Salvation Prayers
- The Race of Faith
- The Macedonian Call Testimony
- God's got a plan
- As He is...So are we
- In good times and bad
- Suffering with Christ
- A Word in Season - A 6 book compilation including:
    - If it's good enough for Jesus…
    - House of Grace
    - Watch and Pray
    - You can do it…in Jesus name!
    - As He is…so are we!
    - The Race of faith